Notes on Corgis Rule! colouring book:

There are 45 pages of unique artwork based on original, hand-drawn Susan Alison corgi designs. The paper in this book is 60lb in weight ie crayons and pencils are your best bet for fab results. It's always a good idea to use a safety sheet underneath each page whatever you're using.

Pictures are only printed on one side of the paper so that you can remove a page and display or frame it without losing the picture on the other side.

I have cropped and enlarged some of the designs to make different pictures and for those who prefer less intricate designs. They also allow experimentation with different colouring schemes. Some I've made into 6"x4" pictures – this is a nice size for framing, or for cutting out and sticking to the front of a greeting card blank. There are also some sheets of notepaper for that special person, and a page of bookmarks that can be coloured and laminated.

At the back of this book are a couple of pages for trying out your colours.

Most importantly – relax and have fun!

To receive advance notice of new books you can subscribe
to my newsletter on any page of my website at:
www.SusanAlison.com

Or just email me at Susan@SusanAlison.com
It's always fab to hear from you!

SUSAN ALISON

CORGIS RULE!

COLOURING BOOK

ISBN-13: 978-1533390752
ISBN-10: 1533390754

website and newsletter sign-up form: www.SusanAlison.com

CONTENTS

Only even numbers appear so that there is no number on the actual picture page. The title of the picture shows opposite the relevant design.

For Melanie

Whose enthusiastic encouragement
for this new venture has been
much appreciated!

Susan Alison

Corgis Rule!

Colouring Book

Butterfly Attraction

Butterfly Attraction

(cropped and enlarged)

Testing, testing

(corgi chef)

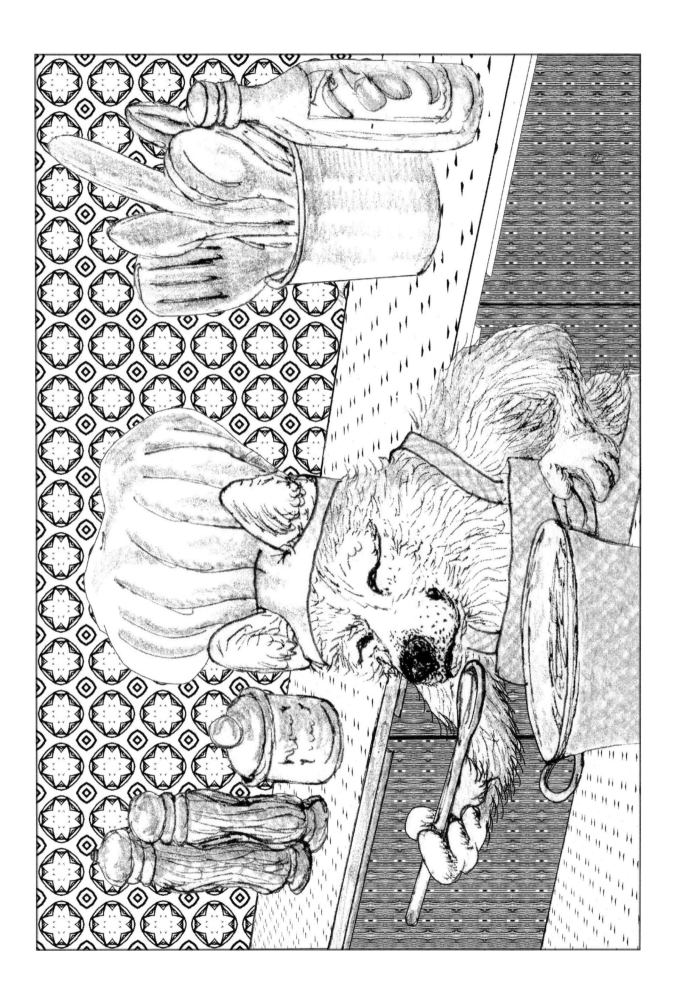

Stained glass corgi

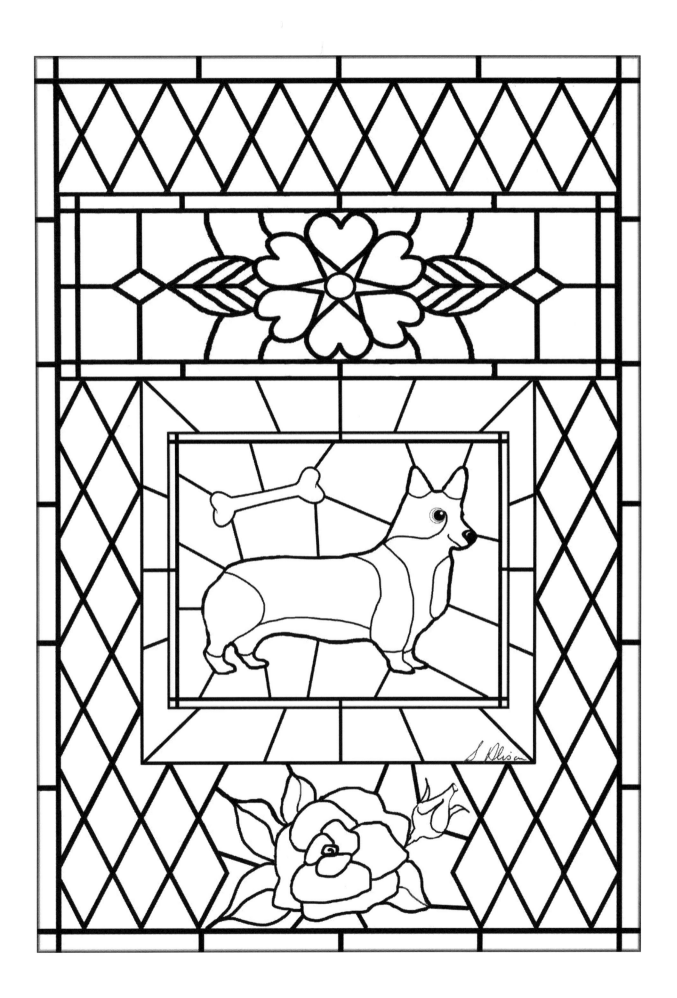

Stained glass corgi

6``x4`` — for framing or for a greeting card front

Or just for colouring!

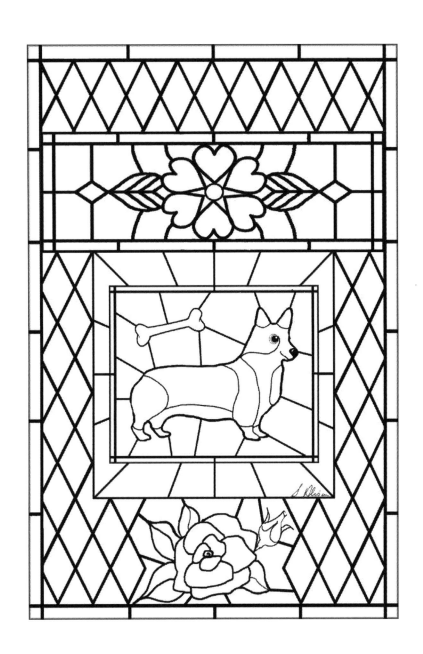

Conan the Corgarian

The Gift

The Gift

(cropped and enlarged)

Rainbow-singers

Rainbow-singers

(with more white space)

Rainbow-singers

6"x4" – for framing or for a greeting card front

Or just for colouring!

Give us a kiss, luv!

Give us a kiss, luv!

(cropped and enlarged)

She was having a duvet day

She was having a duvet day

(cropped and enlarged)

She was having a duvet day

6″x4″ – for framing or for a greeting card front

Or just for colouring!

Corgi Cycle of Life

Save water – bath with your pals

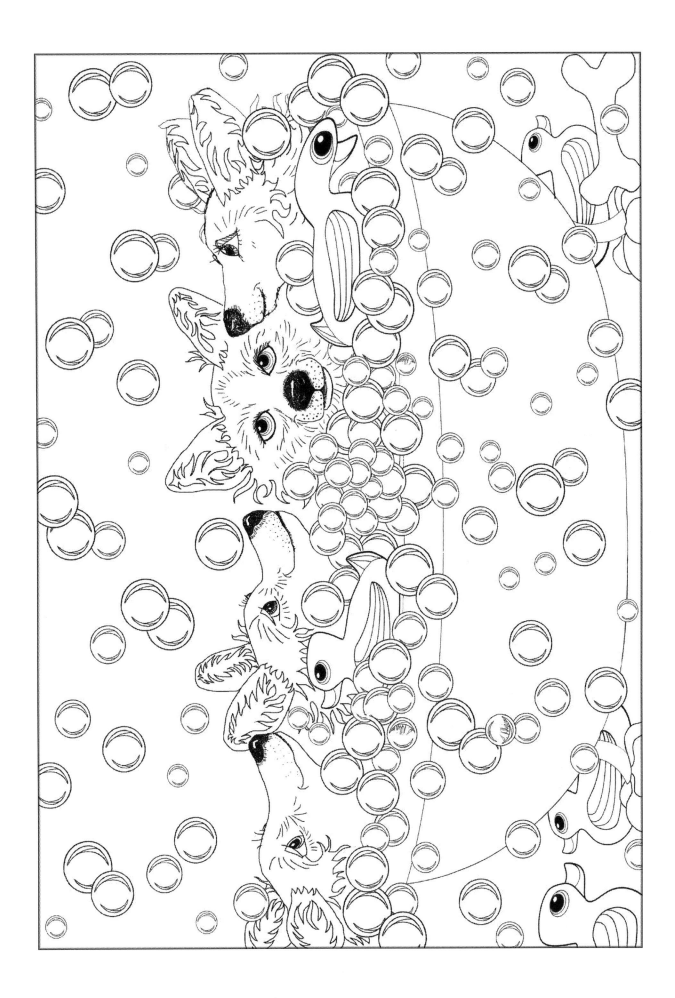

Save water – bath with your pals

(cropped and enlarged)

Save water – bath with your pals

6"x4" – for framing or for a greeting card front

Or just for colouring!

Waiting for the game to start

Waiting for the game to start

(cropped and enlarged)

Waiting for the game to start

6"x4" – for framing or for a greeting card front

Or just for colouring!

Corgiart Nouveau

Corgiart Nouveau

6''x4'' — for framing or for a greeting card front

Or just for colouring!

She loved autumn leaves

She loved autumn leaves

(cropped and enlarged)

She loved autumn leaves

6"x4" — for framing or for a greeting card front

Or just for colouring!

Starry, starry night

Starry, starry night

6"x4" — for framing or for a greeting card front

Or just for colouring!

Christmas tree fairy

Christmas tree fairy

(cropped and enlarged)

Christmas tree fairy

6"x4" — for framing or for a greeting card front

Or just for colouring!

Corgial greetings

68

Corgial greetings

6"x4" — for framing or for a greeting card front

Or just for colouring!

More corgial greetings

Just keeping an eye on things

Just keeping an eye on things

(cropped and enlarged)

Just keeping an eye on things

6"x4" – for framing or for a greeting card front

Or just for colouring!

Notepaper for a special person

'Roses'

Notepaper for a special person

'Star flowers'

Notepaper for a special person

'Teddy'

Bookmarks

'Rose fairies'

'Watching the stars'

'More rose fairies'

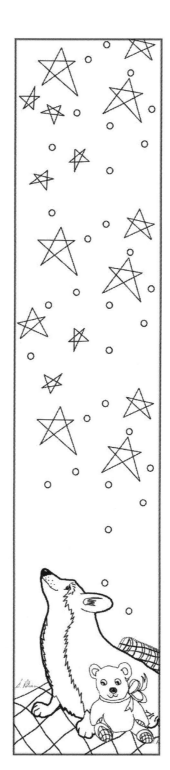

Corgis Rule! Yayyy!!!

A page for trying out your colours:

Another page for trying out your colours:

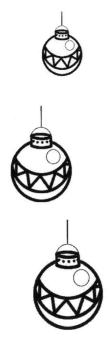

Susan Alison lives in Bristol, UK, and writes and paints full-time. She paints dogs, especially Border Collies, Corgis, Whippets and Greyhounds. Every now and then she paints something that is *not* a dog just to show she's not completely under the paw – mainly, she's under the paw…

Susan's romantic comedies, fantasy novels, illustrated doggerel, short stories; and colouring books can be found on Amazon, Etsy and eBay.

Short stories of hers (*not* usually about dogs) have been published in women's magazines worldwide.

In 2011 she was presented with the Katie Fforde Bursary Award for fiction (with which she's incredibly chuffed).

She has a website at www.SusanAlison.com which features quite a lot of dogs… and if you'd like to receive her (infrequent) newsletter in the comfort of your own inbox, there is a space to put your email address on any of the pages.

Twitter: @bordercollies

Facebook: Susan Alison Art

Also by Susan Alison and available soon...

CAROUSING CATS

Colouring Book (A4 size)
Colouring Book (pocket size)

HOUNDS ABROAD: BOOK THREE

Urban fantasy

The third book starring Lily, Matt and Hounds.

STAKING OUT THE GOAT

Romantic comedy

sequel to the #1 best-selling 'White Lies and Custard Creams'
starring Liz and Moocher.

To receive advance notice of new books you can subscribe
to my newsletter on any page on my website at:
www.SusanAlison.com

Or just email me at Susan@SusanAlison.com
It's always fab to hear from you!

Made in the USA
Columbia, SC
26 August 2020